AMONG THE AMISH

AMONG

THE AMISH

DRAWINGS AND WRITINGS BY KEITH BOWEN

WITH A FOREWORD BY DONALD B. KRAYBILL

RUNNING PRESS

Philadelphia • London

© 1996 by Keith Bowen

Printed in China

9   8   7   6   5   4   3   2   1
Digit on the right indicates the number of this printing

Library of Congress Cataloging-in-Publication Number 96-67132
ISBN 1-56138-747-9

Art direction and design by Ken Newbaker
Edited by Brian Perrin

This book may be ordered by mail from the publisher. Please include $2.50 for postage and handling.
But try your bookstore first!
Running Press Book Publishers
125 South Twenty-second Street
Philadelphia, Pennsylvania 19103-4399

To my brother Colin

CONTENTS

FOREWORD

In this book Keith Bowen takes us on a journey to the heart of Amish society. His sensitive portrayal of Amish life stands apart from the many photography books on the subject. His drawings and paintings capture a community's ways in an exquisite yet intimate fashion.

Bowen's personal warmth, gentleness, and unobtrusive style quickly won the hearts of the Amish people in Lancaster County. They were impressed and delighted by how his hand could record their work and play on paper, and the trust he inspired gave Bowen further access to the many private aspects of Amish life portrayed on the following pages.

The Amish espouse a simple religious faith, humility, obedience, communal values, and separation from the world. Distinctive features of their culture include using a horse and buggy for transportation, wearing distinctive clothing, speaking a German dialect, and using technology selectively.

The Amish trace their roots to the Anabaptists of sixteenth-century Europe. A radical offshoot of the Protestant Reformation, the Anabaptists emphasized adult baptism, pacifism, the separation of church and state, a practical Christian faith, and the importance of community.

Today the Amish number about 150,000 and live in some 225 settlements in twenty-two states and in the Canadian province of Ontario. Despite their traditional ways they have flourished in the midst of modern life. Their families are large, with an average of seven to nine children, and few Amish ever leave the culture to live in the world. As a result, many Amish communities double in population as often as every twenty years.

Guided by religious principles, the Amish interact selectively with the larger society. The Church forbids ownership of automobiles, computers, televisions, and radios. Electricity is not tapped from public utility lines. Amish children attend one-room schools operated by the community. High school is considered unnecessary for a successful life. The Amish worship not in church buildings but in their homes and in the homes of their neighbors, every other Sunday. Twenty-five to thirty-five families typically constitute a church district.

The vignettes in these pages ring with authenticity and integrity. The unfettered narrative enhances the drawings and relates Bowen's encounters with the real people behind the stereotypes of Amish life.

DONALD B. KRAYBILL
MESSIAH COLLEGE
GRANTHAM, PENNSYLVANIA

PREFACE

Back home, in Wales, I'd never heard of the Amish. "Who are they?" was my first reaction to the suggestion that I visit Lancaster County, Pennsylvania, and create a book on the Amish way of life.

I did a little research and asked around. "You won't need to take any colors with you," I was told. "Just a bottle of black ink will do—they only wear black."

On my first day in Lancaster County, some well-meaning locals told me that they had lived in the area for many years and still knew no Amish people. "You'll never get to meet them," they said. "The Amish are too private. Keep themselves to themselves."

I set out to explore the back roads of Lancaster County. The scene came as a shock, a revelation, to me as I turned the corner and saw a small boy in a straw hat working a team of massive brown horses. They moved slowly across the field in the soft autumn sunlight, trailing a plume of golden-red dust that rose into the clear blue sky.

Stunned, I got out of the car and sat by the side of the road, lost in a view that seemed to come from another century. Sometime later I thought I'd better get out my sketchbook and start drawing. That's what I was there for.

In those first few weeks I sat by the side of many roads, drawing farm scenes with distant figures heading in the opposite direction. Then things began to change: an occasional hand would wave to me from inside a passing buggy; children's faces would peek out from the back window, watching me as they moved slowly down the road.

One Sunday afternoon a buggy stopped. The couple inside asked to see my drawings. I handed them the sketchbook, and it disappeared into the darkness of the carriage. The passengers handed it back with questions and kind compliments.

As the weeks went by and I continued to draw—by the side of the road and in the market—more and more Amish approached me and looked on with curiosity. Especially the children. Young boys often followed me around, watching my sketchpad and the movements of my pencil.

Later, I realized that my art—drawing—probably made me less of a threat to the Amish than other non-Amish, or "English," visitors they had seen. Drawing is simple, direct, handmade. You set out your stall for everyone to see, you share something with the onlookers. It's more in keeping with the Amish belief system than photography. You *take* a photograph, but with a drawing you give something back.

Eventually I was formally introduced to Gideon, an Amish gentleman who, I had been told, might be able to introduce me to some local families and help me make more intimate contacts. We sat on opposite sides of an office table. I showed him my drawings and explained my book to him. We arranged to meet a few days later, after he had had some time to think about whether and how he could help. When I met Gideon again, he told me a few families might be willing to talk with me. "Shall we go and visit?" he asked.

Gideon's introductions led to friendships with families and individuals that went far beyond my initial hopes and expectations. Without him and the people he introduced me to, this book would not have been possible.

Over the next couple of years, I made many extended visits to Lancaster County. I spent my days living among the Amish from sunrise to sunset, returning to the "English" world only at night. I spent a lot of time drawing, of course. But in thanks for the hospitality I was shown and to better understand the subject of my drawings, I also joined my new friends in work and play. I learned to fork hay, hang tobacco, plow fields, harvest melons, can fruit, and even race scooters. All of these things the Amish taught me as I worked. But most of all, they taught me to listen in silence and to appreciate the serenity of a lifestyle that has been lost to my world.

Though I asked the Amish many questions about their way of life and their system of beliefs, I made no organized study of their rules or religion. I certainly don't pretend to be an expert. This book is merely a record of my personal encounters with the Amish men, women, and children who have become my friends. Out of respect for their values, I have chosen not to mention their family names. But you don't have to know their names or their rules to appreciate their stories. After all, as one friend told me: "We might dress a little differently, but we're just people, you know."

ACKNOWLEDGMENTS

My sincere thanks to Colin Dougan, Brad Igou, Jerry Irwin, Ed Klimuska, Donald Kraybill, and Phillip Woolley.

AUTUMN

FIRST IMPRESSIONS

The sun is warm today. I sit at the side of the road, drawing the farm buildings opposite. It's one of the last good days before the winds come from the north. My drawing is coming along well.

Hands are raised in greeting from the inside of passing buggies. Later, one of the buggies stops and a couple lean out to ask if they can see my drawing. "How long has it taken? Where are you from?" they want to know. "Thank you for showing us."

A small boy with a battered straw hat comes over from the farm to look at my drawing. His older brother follows and stays to talk. The boys have been left with their three other brothers to look after the farm while their parents are at a wedding. It's November and it's a Tuesday. Weddings are held mostly in November, after the harvest season, on Tuesdays and Thursdays.

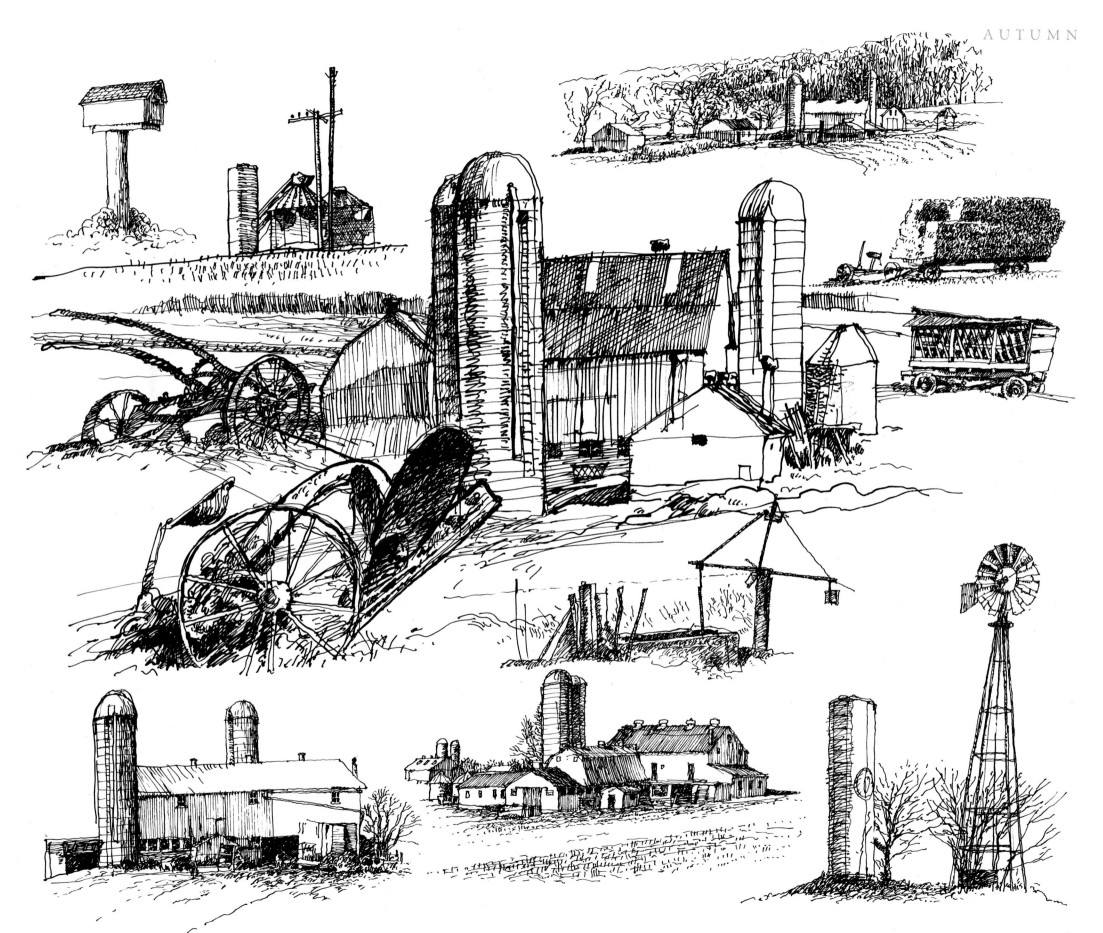

The parents have been away since eight this morning and won't be back until ten tonight. Later in the afternoon the boys bring a bucket of water so I can wash my brushes. Then the eldest brother comes past on an old iron-wheeled tractor, pulling a heavy cart.

He tries to pull the cart up the incline that leads into the barn. After several failed attempts he unhitches the cart and tries to push it through the door, but this also proves useless. Finally, his other brothers and I help pull the cart in as the tractor pushes it from behind. Eventually we succeed. We store the cart in the recesses of the dark barn, under a brown canopy of tobacco leaves.

Today is one of the last warm days of the season. Sitting here in the sun is pleasant, but it's uncomfortably cool on the shady side of the barn. Occasionally a gust of wind blows from the north, a hint of the icy blast that will come in a few weeks to detach the last of the leaves from the almost bare trees.

PICKING CORN

Again I sit by the road, drawing some machinery that's been left at the top of a farm drive. A man comes by in a large cart pulled by two horses. He stops to talk and look at the drawings.

He has seven children—about average for Amish families. The first three are girls, followed by four boys, all between two and twelve. We talk about families, the business of farming, and then his favorite subject: hunting.

He's a hunter. Uses a rifle to hunt buck, which have a very short season of two weeks. When he shoots them, he guts them on the spot, then takes them home on the back of a horse. There he skins them, boils the meat for three hours, and seals it in cans. "There's too much meat to can it all, so with what's left, we take it around to a neighbor and pop it in their freezer," he tells me.

We're joined by another man and a boy who bring a team of four horses and begin hitching them to the

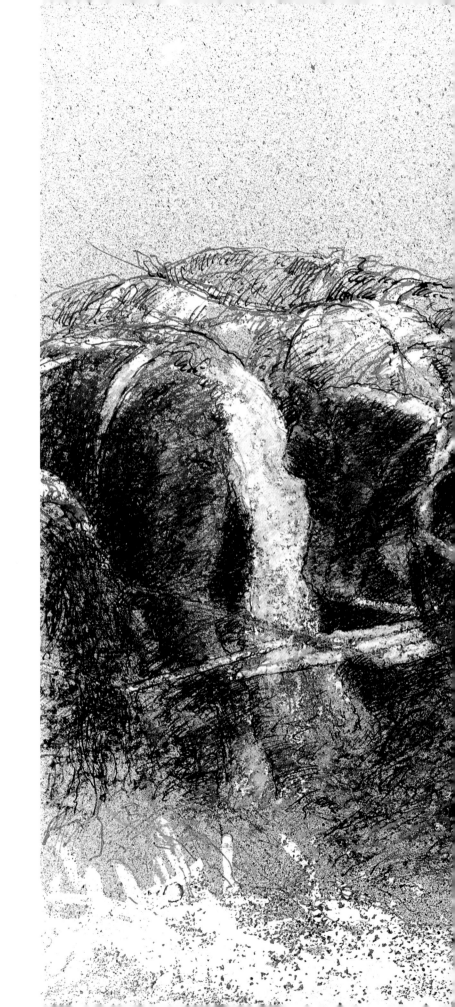

harvester I was drawing. The harness chains are rusty, so the boy pours oil on them once they've been fitted to the horses. Afterward he goes around the back and wipes his oily hands on the horses' tails.

"We're going down to harvest the late corn crop. Would you like to come along and draw us?" the farmer asks.

Down in the fields the breeze blows through the dry corn leaves, rattling them like paper decorations. There's about half an acre of crop left. The horses gradually work their way around it. Four horses pull the harvester, and two more follow slightly behind, pulling the cart to catch the falling cobs. As soon as the first cart is full, another cart comes along to replace it. Meanwhile, the first cart goes back to the barn for unloading.

Slowly, the cart fills with harvested corncobs as the horses pull it around the field. "We'll be done by the end of the week," Jonas tells me.

Up at the barn, the wheels of a tractor have been re-moved. Its driveshaft now turns the belt that runs the elevator taking the corn into the loft. School has finished for the day, so now there are more children helping with the various tasks. I'm sitting opposite the barn, drawing. A crowd of young boys and girls stand a short distance away, watching me intently. I tell them to come over if they want to look, and immediately they're standing at my back, whispering quietly when they recognize the figures in the drawing.

"That's Uncle Jonas," I hear them giggling. They're so polite, so quiet, and so shy.

The children come home from school in the afternoon.
They disappear into the house for about five minutes,
then return to shovel corn off the cart and onto the
elevator that carries it up into the loft.
Later, in the loft, the corn will be
ground up for cattle feed.

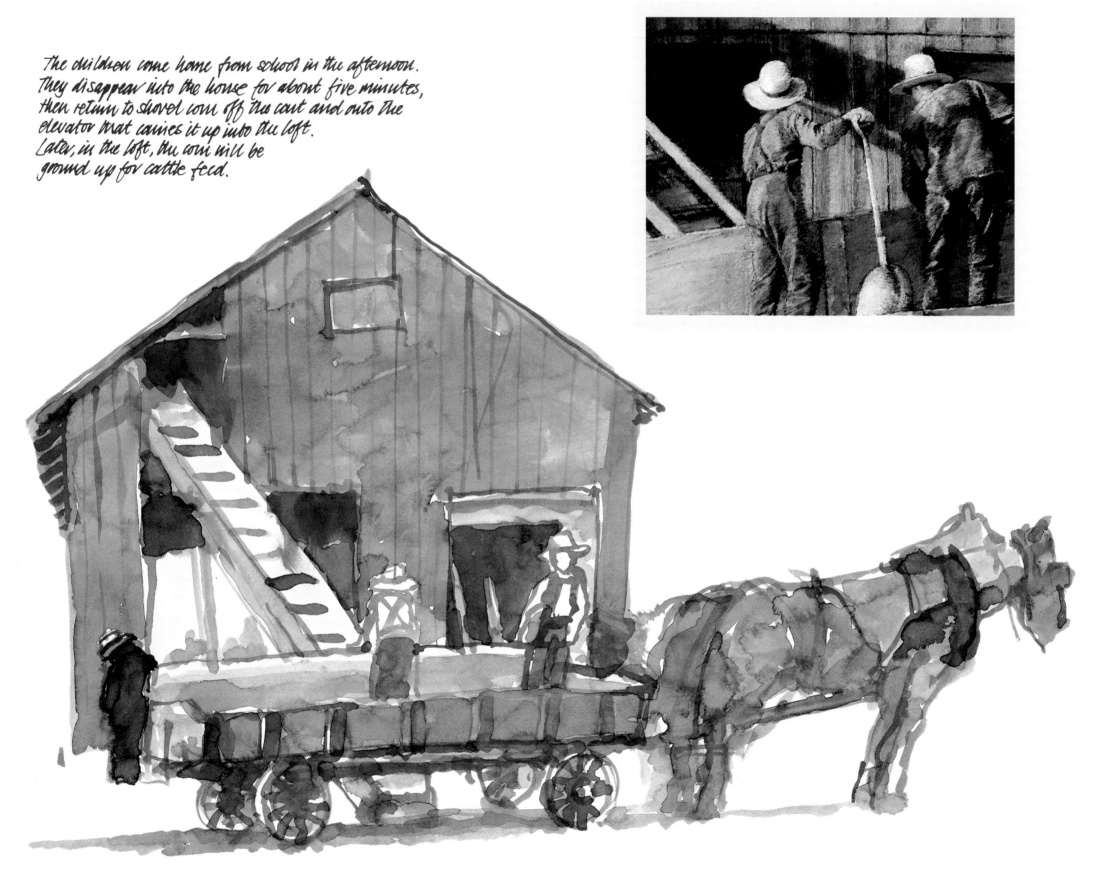

IN THE CARPENTER'S WORKSHOP

This door I'm working on is a love affair," says Christian. "My wife picked it up in a sale somewhere. I'm getting it ready for my son's house. We're here in the workshop 300 days of the year to work. Well, not always to work—sometimes to play."

Farming is no longer always a viable means of making a living because of the high cost of land. Forty percent of the Lancaster County Amish community no longer work at full-time farming. A significant number work in the building industry.

Christian gives me a tour of his workshop. "A table saw is to a carpenter as a Bible is to a preacher." (Christian is fond of analogy.) "Now this jointer saw is pretty good—maybe a little shaky, but we're not working on a government project. This isn't for the White House. It's just for my place," he says, holding up another door panel.

"Did a job for a doctor on Long Island once. He paid well, and when we delivered we saw he had two Rolls-Royce cars. And all these animal heads all over the place—moose heads, bear heads, all sorts." Was he a hunter? "Either that or a butcher!"

Christian laughs. "Now, an Amish farmer I know bought his seven children—three girls and four boys—a farm each. He doesn't farm particularly well, but he must be doing something right!"

Christian wanders across the workshop toward me, unrolling a set of plans and laying them open across a table. "This is the blueprint for the cabinet," he explains. "Now what do you think is the most important thing when making a cabinet?" I don't know. Christian's face lights up: "The checkbook, of course."

In the cellar is the "engine house," where a diesel motor drives the generator that powers all the tools. Upstairs, in the "drawing office," all of the latest plans and commissions are spread out on tables. At the far end of the workshop is a sign explaining office hours: "Lately I've been here just about all the time, except when I'm someplace else."

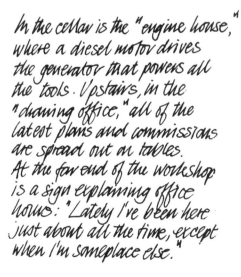

WEDDINGS

We drive past an Amish farm. "There's going to be a wedding there soon," Gideon tells me. How do you know that? I wonder. He points out a row of celery stalks, still in the soil, that are wrapped to protect them from the frost. Creamed celery is a main dish at weddings.

Married couples don't wear wedding rings. After the wedding, the bride and groom spend the winter visiting and staying with all of their guests. During this time, they receive gifts to start their own house.

Though they stay together through the visiting period, husband and wife do not move into a house of their own until the spring. Moving day is usually about the first of April. "Well, it used to be, in my day," an elderly Amish gentleman explains. "Maybe it's a little different today."

SUPPERTIME

Many trees have fallen in a recent storm. They need to be cleared. Emmanuel is using the chain saw while Alan, his son, operates the hydraulic wood splitter. Back at their farm, Isaac, one of Alan's younger brothers, has the job of operating the lever while Alan feeds in the blocks of cut wood. Emmanuel hoists up another tree that has crashed through a fence. "There must have been something wrong with this tree for it to have come down in the gale," he says. "Look how rotten it is in the middle."

After another load of firewood is brought home, we are called in for supper. We wash our hands, and the men hang up their hats and comb their hair. We sit at the table, everyone chattering happily. It's six o'clock. Sarah is asking me how my watch works, since there is no handle to wind it up. I tell her that it works by the movement of my arm, which keeps the motor going inside—it has no battery. "But does it stop when you sleep?" she asks.

The Amish don't wear wristwatches. Daniel says he doesn't carry a pocket watch, since it won't work with him. "It must be the electricity in me. We're on a different time than you—slow time, farmers' time. When I'm in the fields I can hear the whistle from the hat shop. It goes off at twelve o'clock. I know to break then."

Suddenly, everyone is quiet, even the very young ones, as Emmanuel bows his head in silent prayer. For a few minutes in a busy day, the family prays together before starting to eat the meal.

The table is laden with food. A salad of minced carrot, plates of fried chicken, bowls of mashed potato, sweet corn, beans, and applesauce. Each plate is loaded with food, eaten, and cleaned off with a spoon, ready for the next course: yogurt, pumpkin pie, hot apples, and tapioca, all washed down with glasses of water.

Supper is soon over. Nobody lingers at the table; everyone has work to get back to. Even the small boys have their jobs to do. This evening, five-year-old Isaac has to sweep the dairy floor. The girls clean up the dishes, then go back into the fields to pick beans until dark. Emmanuel remarks to me as the shadows begin to lengthen: "You see, my wife's out there now picking beans. Plenty of protein there. She's really mad on them. Picks them every evening until the frosts come."

Sunday

The bench wagon is parked at the back of the farm. It holds all the books, plates, and benches for a church service. It moves every other Sunday from one house to another, clockwise around the church district. In other districts it moves counter-clockwise, but nobody seems to know why.

Tidying up and cleaning has been going on for the last couple of weeks. The room dividers are pushed back to allow the chairs to be arranged for the service. There will be seating for about fifty people.

A table is set in the kitchen for the men, and another for the women in a room on the other side of the wall. The table setting is quite particular, with a cup and saucer, water glass, and knife at each place, plus a pile of knives placed in the center. There are no forks or spoons, though I did hear one elderly man reminding a group of women to make sure they put a fork at his place.

In the middle of the table are jars of peanut butter, crab-apple jelly, cheese spread, pickles, and beets, and plates of butter, cheese, bologna, and bread. In all, twenty-four loaves of bread have been baked fresh by five different women. And then, of course, there are the pies: thirty-five total, all baked yesterday afternoon. There are twenty-eight schnitz pies and seven apple. These have been stacked on the portable wooden pie shelves, ready for tomorrow.

Things will start at half past four tomorrow morning, with the milking and feeding to be done before breakfast

"Behold, how good
and pleasant it
is for brethren
to dwell together
in unity."
Psalms 133:1

and then a wash and change of clothes before the worshipers start arriving at about seven o'clock. The service starts at eight.

The church visits each house about once every six months. An upcoming church visit is an occasion for house-cleaning and garden upkeep. The women prepare food because after the three-hour service the day becomes a social event.

I sit with Elias during lunch. He explains to me that his church district's boundaries are drawn on all sides of his land. None of the neighbors we can see are in the same church as his family.

"Our church is small, only about forty people. As soon as it gets bigger than about ninety, we divide the congregation. You see, there are just too many people to fit into the house." There are several ministers, deacons, and a bishop to lead the congregation in services.

After the meal some people go off visiting, while relatives often stay for most of the day. "On our Sunday off, we visit other churches. We can also visit other churches even when it's our Sunday to worship, but we mostly prefer to be with our own church."

23

WINTER

THE WATER WHEEL

We always had good fresh water to drink," my friend Gideon tells me of his parents' farm. "There were times the wheel stopped—when there was flood water in the winter covering the wheel, or when it was frozen, covered in ice and frozen fast to the frame. We'd have to go and loosen it by cutting the ice with a hatchet, or cover the boards around the wheel with corn fodder to keep out the cold.

"The water ran by gravity into the horse-watering trough in the forebay, then into the trough in the manure yard for the cattle to drink. The overflow went to the sheep stable and over along into the creek. There was very little water running out there, since the wheel could be regulated to run faster or slower."

How do you control it? I ask.

"You know, the wire should be tight from the wheel, across the fields, to the pump at the well, so that the pulling action is efficient. The looser the wire, the less movement you have at the top. That's the balance."

Another storm is forecast for this evening. We pick up the children and the teacher from the school. Driving down the lanes as the flurries begin, we stop to let the passengers out one by one. The last to leave are two small boys. They get out of the carriage just as the snow reaches near-blizzard pitch. They say thank you, wrap their scarves tightly around their heads to hold their hats on, and head down the snowy path to the front door. "Don't worry about them," Gideon tells me. "In a quarter of an hour they'll be back out to play, completely covered in snow."

THE HORSE AUCTION

I'm going to tell you what Dan told me they are," the auctioneer patters on. "The first horse here is a six-year-old. He come right off the track a week ago out of Florida. He's broke now, one hundred percent. Now, Dan has the papers for this horse. As far as he knows he's traffic safe and sound and okay. A pretty nice horse right here. Let's get it over before he gets here. He might call at any time."

His flow is uninterrupted as two more horses are led out of the marquee, past the men standing at its entrance, and trotted up and down the road for the crowd to view.

It's a bright, sunlit morning. The temperature is well below freezing. Big, thick yellow gloves and short-cut Wellington boots appear to be standard protection against the cold and damp. The gloves, in spite of their color, are apparently acceptable—not too "worldly."

In one nearby tent a quilt auction continues at a fast clip. In another, two Amish auctioneers work through various lots of antiques and bric-a-brac.

The hot-pretzel van is doing a brisk business. People young and old stand around talking and eating. I understand the reason for the boots—mud is everywhere, inside and outside the tents.

Another horse is run up and down the street, the auctioneer's voice ringing through the clear winter air: "Here's a mare that'll do somebody a lot of good, a real horse. Eight years old, just shipped, acclimated, been in the carriage."

The hammer comes down in the next tent. Another lot has been sold.

"He's five years old, been on a Mennonite farm in Union Town. Born there. Hitched a few times. Never

asked to do much, but does drive. Never had shoes on him. Five years old. Never asked to do a whole lot, but knows a little somethin' when it comes to hooking up. Just take him home and break him the way you want him. He's awake. Got a lot of life. Five years old. All of life in front of him."

"Can you put the shoes on?" comes the question from the crowd.

"I got enough to do putting my own on in the morning. Never been spoilt. Never been asked to do it. I know where the horse came from."

The bidding is brisk, with the auctioneer pleading: "Don't move around too much, 'cause I don't know who's in if you move around too much."

✦ ✦

My friend Emmanuel, who brought me to the auction, tells me a joke:

An Amish man goes along to an auction to bid on a farm. His final bid, $42,000, is successful. He returns home and tells his wife to fetch the tin with the money from the cellar. She brings it up, and they start to count the dollars. When it's all been carefully counted, the Amish man scratches his head. "That's funny," he says. "Why, there's only $38,000 in this tin." He looks puzzled, then turns to his wife: "Take it back. The $42,000 must be in the other tin."

Men young and old line the road to watch
the horses run back and forth. Around
the back of the marquee, some young
women, bundled against the cold, eat
hot pretzels and drink — of all things —
ice-cold canned drinks.

SPREADING MANURE

There are three things a man does in the winter," Samuel tells me. "Reads his Bible, loves his wife, and hauls manure—not necessarily in that order, of course.

"Most of it is spread in winter, before the spring planting. We spread it wherever we can: on the alfalfa patch, in the neighbor's flower garden, and over any visiting artists.

"Box-stall manure—you know, from the heifers, horses, goats, steers, or whatever—is chunky stuff. It'll fly around when you spread it. It's also not so polluting. But pit manure, that's something else. That's evil stuff. We clear the tank once, sometimes twice, a year. It's a liquid. Oh, the smell! That's when you get trouble with the neighbors."

The morning is cold and clear. Milking is over and the milking parlor has been cleaned out. One of the horses stands on a platform that extends out of the back of the parlor. He's enjoying the sunshine, looking down at me quizzically as I wander past. Soon his rest period will be over and he'll have to haul another load of manure out onto the fields.

After spreading manure, Samuel loads a cart with bales of hay to take to the animals in the barn.

THE FARM AUCTION

I t's the day before the big farm-machinery auction. As I survey the scene, more and more massive trucks arrive, carrying pieces of extraordinary farm implements. "Some of these trucks have taken two or three days to get here with their loads," someone tells me.

I notice that the large cranes used to move the machinery off the trucks and into line have rubber tires. I ask one of the Amish men involved in the work how this is possible, since only metal wheels are normally permitted on fields. "Oh, this auction is special," he tells me, "so the Church has allowed us to use cranes with rubber wheels."

◆ ◆

The straw hats and the black hats all look the same today—a translucent, milky-white color. They're covered with a see-through plastic, elasticized to fit over the top and down around the brim—to protect against the weather.

In the morning the organizer has his initials drawn on a piece of paper and attached to his jacket by a large safety

Some items on the printed handout at the auction:
Tractors — Belly Mower
New Equipment: Milk Sputnik, Grim Hay Tedder,
Horse Drawn Ice Saw
At the bottom, referring to the steam engine, the legend
is inscribed: "The fender man will be here."

pin. But later, in the afternoon, this is changed, and a new plastic-covered paper notice is now stuck into the band of his hat at the front. This time the initials are bigger.

It snows, then it sleets. Black umbrellas proliferate to shield against the driving ice.

Despite the hundreds of black-Wellington-booted feet that have tramped back and forth across the snow, only at the edges, by the road, has the ground turned to an orange-brown mud. The ice and snow persist, providing a stark contrast to the machinery and moving black figures.

The auctioneers move efficiently down the aisles of stacked machinery, quickly dispensing one lot after another. One more deal is closed, and the successful bidder reaches a hand into his jacket to pull out and show an orange card with his registration number, boldly inscribed.

At the edges of the crowd, small groups stand and chat, or look over some piece of equipment, pulling and pushing its various levers. Then they shuffle away.

The sleet has stopped, but now the wind picks up. Most of the people seem to be wearing only their short jackets; few overcoats are in evidence. They stand hunched over, shirt collars up and hands forced deeper and deeper into pockets as they feel the bite of the bitter wind. But I have noticed a couple of concessions to warmth and comfort: an astounding pair of yellow gloves, a bright-red scarf, and a pair of fluffy earmuffs (black, of course) under one young man's hat.

My initial impression of black uniformity changes as I walk around and begin to make out various individuals. Then I recognize Alvin, whom I met yesterday. He's still in his late teens or early twenties, and married, with a baby boy. I watch as he jumps onto the back of an open truck, crouching down out of the wind and pulling his collar up and his straw hat down. He lives nearby, so he'll be back home and out of the cold very soon.

I am drawing a group of four young men who, quite unusually, are wearing long raincoats and puffing on large cigars while checking over a rake. The head of the group is stockily built with a broad, pockmarked face. This is his day out with his friends.

Later, I sit on a wooden pallet, drawing a steam engine, dipping my brush into puddles of melted snow. A

loft above and scattered on the newly swept yard. The game is on: Amish versus Team Mennonite.

I go into the barn and up to the loft to look at the yard below. Here in the loft are Amish and Mennonite girls together, sporting small, fringed shoulder bags with a selection of attached buttons. One of them reads: LOVE IS THE BEST THING. The girls are crowded around the openings, giggling and talking quietly to each other, looking at the game below, looking at the boys.

Back downstairs, where there are only men and boys, there's a striking lack of noise for such a large gathering. I work my way through the crowd into a far corner where I can draw unnoticed. There's little hope of this—I'm the only splash of Gore-Tex blue in a sea of heavy black cotton serge. A little boy has followed me and now sits on the gate behind me, fascinated by every move of the pencil.

To play the game, four boys from one team spread out into each corner of the yard. Two boys from the opposing team stand in the center. The four boys at the corners pass the ball three times. After the third pass, the boy who has the ball tries to hit one of the boys in the center. If a center boy is hit, he drops out; otherwise the thrower drops out.

The ball goes around and across from each corner, the boys feigning throws at the center. One tactic seems to be to look at the boy in the center, fix his gaze, and pretend you're about to throw the ball at him. Then, without altering your gaze, you throw to the other corner.

The sound of the ball being caught—high-velocity leather on naked skin—is testimony to its speed through the air. No catcher's mitt for this lot. Alvin says the ball is made of cowhide and stitched, but he doesn't know what's inside. "It's not so painful when it hits you," he says stoically. Then I overhear someone saying a boy once had his nose broken when the ball hit his face.

The boys in the middle adopt a stooped gait, ducking away and trying to anticipate the next throw. They jump high off the ground, curving their backs to narrowly avoid the ball, and crash down on the straw with both feet still in the air.

One of the Amish players, a boy in a vivid green shirt, carries the art of the feigned throw to new levels of

man with a little boy comes across to me: "Hope you don't mind us coming over to look?" They stand peering down at the drawing, the man holding the boy's hand.

Do you like to draw? I ask the little boy. He nods. "But we always run out of paper," his father says. "My name's Aaron." He squats down beside me, with the boy standing close, his hand still safely in his father's. Aaron tells me of this summer's tobacco harvest and the corner ball game tomorrow: "It'll be in that yard where the cows are now. They'll clean it and throw straw down." All the time we are talking, father and son hold hands—a large, rough, hard, earth-colored hand gently clasping one that is small, soft, and pale.

Next day, as it comes to afternoon, the crowd throng around the barn and yard. They're ready for the corner ball, or *ecke balle*, game. Straw bales are hurled from the

theatricality. His left hand slaps his leg as the right hand waves above his head, propelling the deadly ball to lock onto its next target with laserlike precision. His best trick is to catch and throw the ball with his right hand in one sweeping, uninterrupted movement. Somebody should sign this boy up.

Occasionally the ball lands in the mud that surrounds the yard. It's retrieved quickly and cleaned with handfuls of straw by each corner as he throws it around.

Another bale of straw is dropped from the loft, creating a brief flurry of straw bits that land gently on the rows of black hats and shoulders. I'm still tucked away in my spot at the back of the crowd, drawing. People notice me from time to time, then turn their attention back to the game. A Mennonite man turns around to joke: "Can you draw them while they jump?"

Now an elderly Amish man comes over. As he looks through the drawings, recognizing himself, I ask him to explain the game. The little boy still sits on the gate behind me, transfixed by my pencil moving across the paper. Some older boys have joined him. They want to know whether the game will be on television. I look puzzled. "Your drawings—they say you're from the television." Still puzzled, I reply, No, they're just going to be in this sketchbook. That's all. They don't seem convinced. The elderly Amish man smiles gently by my side.

On the last day of the auction, there are very few Amish around—mostly just visitors like myself from outside the community, whom the Amish call "English." The Amish aren't particularly interested in antiques or tractors, and those are the items on today's agenda. The atmosphere—especially the clothing—is quite a contrast to the previous day. The barn is closed, and the yard where the corner ball game was played is now deserted. A few plodding cows drink from the puddles of melted ice.

THE CARRIAGE WORKSHOP

There are about eight carriage shops in Lancaster County, but probably more down around Nine Points that I don't know of," Jacob tells me.

I've been visiting the carriage workshop for the past three days, sitting in various corners, drawing away. "Oh, you're from England," the men say on the first day, seeming slightly unsure about just where that is. The second day, they introduce me to another young man: "This is Keith. He's an artist. He comes from . . . where did you say you were from, Poland?"

I notice a brown cardboard box on one of the shelves. The words JAMIE WYETH SLEIGH are printed in bold letters on the side. I ask Jacob about it. "Oh, yes," he says. "About six years ago it was brought in. We repaired it here. Yes, that's right. Now that you mention it, I think he was an artist, too—if I remember rightly."

As I leave I notice a box tacked up beside the doorway. There are two horizontal slots cut side by side in the lid. Inscribed on the lid is a message: "If you have enjoyed your visit to this workshop, place money in the left-hand slot. If you have not, place money in the right-hand slot."

From his wheelchair, Leon puts all his effort into rubbing down, and finishing the cabinets. At the end of the day he moves over to the compressed-air-line to blow off the day's dust, slowly puts on his jacket, hat, and gloves, picks up his lunchbox, and manoeuvres over towards the door.

He climbs out of his wheelchair and onto a small tractor, the engine starts up, and he's off home down the track.

TRAVEL

Returning home from market one day, we come to a fork in the road. Which one shall we take? I ask. "They're both the same, so it doesn't matter," Gideon replies. "Shall I tell you how I know? Well, once I tied a piece of rag to one of the wheels of the buggy and counted the revolutions. Same number of revolutions for both roads. They're both the same."

For longer trips and special occasions—when they take the elderly to Florida or Arizona to spend the winter, for instance—the Amish sometimes hire minibuses. Of course, they also travel by train. One Amish man I met even extolled the delights of meeting fellow travelers at the pool table during a transatlantic journey on the QE2.

I spoke to an airline pilot who told me he had once worked with an Amish copilot. "He visited his family regularly. They accepted it. He just had the flying bug." One wonders how he got the "flying bug" in the first place, being Amish.

"What does it feel like to be above the clouds?" Emmanuel asks me, wanting to know what it's like to fly. He says his four-year-old daughter, Ruth, asked if I had come to visit them in an airplane or a balloon. Unfortunately, I did not come in a balloon.

An Amish woman I met told me she once had to travel briefly to the Midwest. Worried about leaving her mother alone, she reasoned that she would shorten her time away by taking an airplane. Not bothering to consult the Church, she made the trip; upon her return, she told her friends how marvelous it was above the clouds, with the deep blue sky all around and sunshine—bright sunshine—everywhere. She couldn't stop telling people how wonderful it had all been, and, of course, she said that she had returned much sooner to her mother.

Eventually the Church got wind of her adventure, and she was visited by a group of elders who weren't as ecstatic about the flight as she. Later, when she had been censured, some friends asked her whether she would ever do it again. "Oh yes," she eagerly replied. "Tomorrow."

THE COMMUNITY TELEPHONE

Seth's telephone is a field away—around the back of the machine shop, under the electric wire, past the calves and heifers, through a gap in the fence, inside a little booth tucked discreetly among the trees. The booth is made of wood, lined with some type of old silvery insulation and peppered with dog-eared business cards and scribbled numbers.

Sometimes when I'm out in the fields I hear the phone ringing away among the trees. Nobody comes to answer it, of course; nobody can hear it. It always seems pointless to me, until one day when Seth mentions I can always phone him and let him know about any plans I might be making.

But nobody ever answers the phone, I tell him. "Just leave a message," Seth replies. "We've got voice mail here, too, you know. I'll get back to you."

FUNERALS

We're going down the farm drive, with a young mother and child sitting in the back of the buggy. We're off to buy some flowers for her to give her husband on his birthday. As we get to the bottom of the drive, a carriage comes by—a common-enough sight.

"They'll be coming back from a funeral," the young mother remarks. I'm puzzled; how could she possibly know? "Look at the chalked number on the side of the carriage. It's put on when they join the parking line."

Numbered carriages are necessary at large gatherings, where there could be well over a hundred buggies, every one of them identical. And since it is December and not November, they can't be coming from a wedding.

On another day, I see a funeral procession making its way down the road. At its head is a slow-moving carriage with flashing lights, followed by a seemingly never-ending line of buggies. As the procession passes I count more than eighty teams. Later I hear of the funeral of a well-loved bishop, some years before, when there had been a procession of more than three hundred teams.

AT PLAY

I walk past the school. The children are playing outside. Some of the girls are hiding around the corner of the building, playing hide-and-seek, while at the front a bigger boy is shouting at a smaller one, trying to take something from him.

"You can't have that until you're eighteen," he yells.

I wonder what it is.

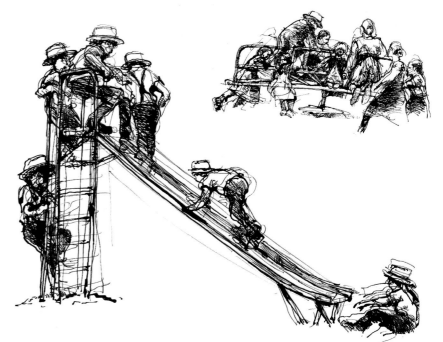

49

"One should keep to old roads and old friends."
German proverb

VISITING

We are visiting friends, going down the drive to the farm. As we drive under a line of washing hung out to dry, Gideon smiles and says, "Did you know the Amish use solar dryers?"

Esther asks what we've both been up to. Oh, just having lunch and visiting, we tell her. "Ah, right, you are being friends today," she replies.

The next place we visit, we end up in the kitchen going through a box of drawings by an Amish artist. The discussion centers on a particular feature of one of the barns that has been altered since the drawing was made. Abner says, "I'd sure like a painting of the barn as it is now." He's still looking down at the drawing. The tone of his voice changes as he hints, "And you wouldn't have to be Amish to do it." I promise to return later with my paints.

SPRING

RETURNING TO EMMANUEL AND SADIE'S

After being away all winter, I'm once again walking down Emmanuel and Sadie's farm drive. It's a fine, sunny spring day. The wash is blowing on the line high above. Everything is the same, just as it should be.

"It's Keith. He's back," says Emmanuel. "You should have been here over the winter. We were thinking about you. You could have made some good drawings. We slaughtered a pig in the barn."

Later, the teacher calls at the house. It's been pets day at school. She stands in the door, holding her baby nephew—her contribution for the day. She's called to tell us that Isaac's cat is stuck behind the stove. Alan and I are dispatched to rescue the cat.

The school is closed, but Alan knows how to ease open the basement door with his penknife. We go up into the schoolroom through the trapdoor—my first and somewhat unique entrance to this particular establishment. After about five minutes we manage to extricate Isaac's cat. Alan wraps the now dusty white cat in his vest, and we go back through the trapdoor.

My first visit to the schoolhouse is not to visit a class in progress but to retrieve Isaac's cat—she's stuck behind the stove. After we rescue her, Alan comforts the frightened, dusty creature.

GOING TO SCHOOL

Since I've been away, Ruth has started school. I ask her mother how Ruth likes it. "She loves it. She walks with the other children along the road. But the cats miss her. After she's fed them in the morning I have to keep them in, or they'd follow her."

The next day, I'm invited to visit the one-room school. There are twenty-five pupils all told, but today only the older ones are in, for test day. Silence reigns as they work away on their papers, seated at the old polished-wood-and-wrought-iron desks.

At 11:15 there's a break. The teacher calls quietly to one group to get their lunch boxes from the cupboards and a cup of water from the sink. Then the other group.

The children sit down, now at different desks—the boys in one corner, the girls in the other. They say a prayer, then start eating and chatting; a few at a time come around to look at the drawings I've made, trying to identify each other.

At 11:40 some go out to play, some carry on with their tests. But they're all back inside by noon. The teacher rings the bell on her desk, and all is immediately silent.

By three o'clock the tests are over, all handed in. The children clean up, then stand to sing a song before going home. "See you, teacher!" they call out as they leave. The teacher does not give homework. The children are expected to complete everything in school so they'll have time at home for house and farm work.

The next day, the pupils have to clean the school to make it ready for the parents-day picnic tomorrow. Outside, some of the children begin mowing the lawns, trimming the edges, raking gravel, and even washing the roof of the outhouse. Inside, others clean the hamster cage while still others sweep the floors and straighten the room, cleaning desks, blackboards, and windows. Buckets, mops, soap, rags, and brushes all are brought to bear with gusto. "It's not usually as noisy as this," the teacher apologizes, turning to me.

At 11:15 they all stand and sing a song, then the boys are pushed outside. "Why can't we stay, teacher?" they complain.

"Because the girls won't be able to mop the floor with the boys around."

The disgruntled boys sit on the porch to put on their rollerblades. A van goes past, dropping newspapers at the

School-room wall-poster:

May your life be like arithmetic—
Friends added,
Enemies subtracted,
Sorrows divided,
Joys multiplied."

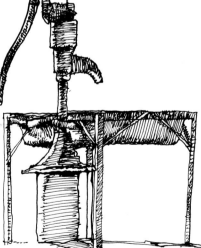

farm entrance opposite. The boys shoot over, spread the papers out, kneel by the roadside to read, then replace the papers carefully before skating off down the road.

As the boys look back at the schoolhouse, the door flies open and another bucket of dirty, soapy water is thrown out. There is some serious floor-mopping going on in there.

When the girls have finished, they also put on their rollerblades and skate away.

"You'll never see an Amish on a bike," Gideon tells me. "It just never got started. You know how resistant we are to change – a little bit here, a little bit there, and before you know it things are out of control. Scooters came along after the Mennonites started riding bicycles. Some did complain, but people looked the other way, and now they're here to stay. Roller skates and rollerblades, too. I think it's okay."

After school some of the children will around outside. A few of the boys take up an informal game of catch.

BARN RAISING

The men arrive around eight o'clock, after they've finished the morning milking. The scene is a flurry of activity.

"The fire destroyed the barn," they tell me. "It was arson. Some kid did it. He lit two barns that night. Wasn't quite right in the head. You know what they say: 'His elevator didn't quite go to the top floor.' It was a big barn, but we'll have it back up in ten days or so."

"Each barn raising has a different flow to it," one man says. "Like I said, if it's arson, then everyone just gets on with it. We have to get the thing up and get the cattle back in. But if someone's building an extension or something a little more relaxed, then you'll get a bit of horseplay coming in. You've seen it, you know what it's like—everybody's busy all over the place. One man's kneeling down while the next guy's nailing his shoe or his pants to the boards. That's always going on. Then there're the daredevils, playing see-saw with a length of board out on the top of the roof. Did you draw that?"

✦ ✦

Lunch is held in the long shed, where tables have been arranged. The women go back and forth with food from the house. To accommodate all of the men, two sittings are held. The men line up to wash their hands and face before eating, laying their hats on the grass.

By five o'clock most of the men are setting off home for the evening milking. Some are still high up, straddling a support beam, nailing up the sheathing boards.

HARROWING

A young boy, about ten, is patiently leading a team of six horses, a harrow, and a roller in ever-shrinking circles around a plowed field. The circle of unharrowed soil is a lighter reddish-brown. It grows smaller and smaller, ceding to the darker soil, until it finally disappears and the job is complete.

The boy leads the team to the edge of the field and un-hitches the roller and harrow, leaving two horses in the field while he leads the other four out onto the road. Traffic is beginning to bear down on him as he reins the four horses down the road. The remaining two horses, who were supposed to stay in the field, come out, cross the road, and follow him.

There isn't much the boy can do now. The traffic is right behind him. He must continue the two hundred yards to the farm gate. The horses behind him are forcing the pace, anxious to be back to their stables.

As the boy passes me, I'm acutely aware of the danger he faces—one small boy sandwiched among four large, heavy, trotting horses, fighting for control of the reins; two horses following, loose, behind him; behind the horses a line of impatient traffic. The horses steadily increase their pace, and I watch with relief as the whole group turns swiftly into the farmyard and out of danger.

CORN PLANTING

Everyone's planting corn in Lancaster County right now. Leave your car there and they'll plant right over it," someone tells me.

Samuel's harrowing before planting corn. A plume of reddish-brown dust blows away from him across the field. The harrow is new, but the oak roller seems to be from a bygone age.

From a distance, Samuel appears to bounce gently across the field while holding onto the reins. Sometimes he stands upright on the bar at the front of the harrow, leaning back gently on the reins for balance. It looks difficult. Samuel says, grinning, "I didn't learn it in a day."

PICNICKING

We are sitting in the corner of a field. The barn swallows swoop and dive overhead. We're taking a break during corn planting— Emmanuel and Sadie, their children Linda, Michael, Ruth, Alan, Isaac, and Elmer, and I. Sadie has brought the food out on a little wagon with small rubber wheels: cold meats, cheeses, grapes, and watermelon. Emmanuel is asking me about my drawings.

"Maybe we don't see what's so interesting. It takes someone from away to see it for us. What's your weather like at home?"

Our winters are not as cold as yours, I tell him. And our summers are not as hot. Your winter, this year, was so cold; we just don't have winters like that.

"No," Alan says with a grin, standing up and eating a piece of watermelon, "we don't usually have winters like that either."

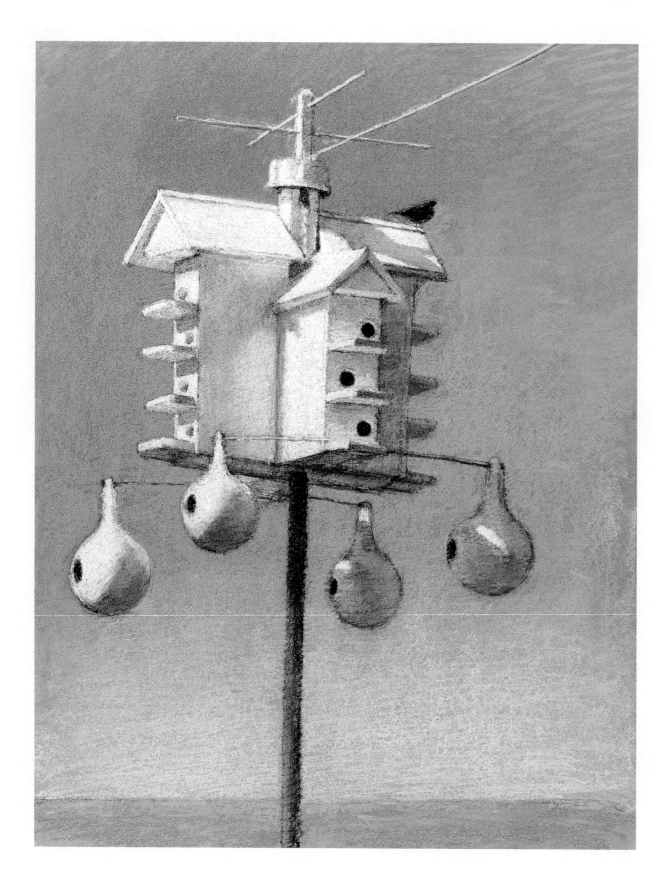

MARTIN HOUSES

Having martin houses is purely practical—the birds eat enormous quantities of flying insects, including mosquitoes. They also drive away hawks and crows. This is beneficial to all during the summer months. Besides, as Emmanuel says, "They sound real nice."

At the beginning of the season, the martin houses take a lot of work. They must be cleaned, and the sparrows must be kept out.

The martin is a social bird, preferring to live in large colonies, and likes to be near farm animals and people. Its natural nesting site is usually the hollow of a dead tree.

In early spring the martins migrate north. A male martin scout flies ahead to look for a suitable house. Many families live in one house. It has to be big enough—with several apartments for each family—clean and white, high up, with open space around and no trees near.

The belief is that the more martins there are flying around, the happier the farmer and his family will be.

QUILTING

Emma is sitting by her quilting frame, singing softly. She is a young woman with a lovely voice. The room is quiet, with just the sound of the clock chiming every hour. Her husband, Amos, and an elderly Amish man come into the room to look at my drawing. "You've got that just right," they say.

Emma tells me how she pricks her finger with the needle to know when it's come through the cloth. I tell her of the old Amish lady who told me about putting a dab of nail polish on her finger to stop the pricking. Emma hasn't heard of that one and seems a little unsure about just what nail polish is.

She tells me how wonderful her grandmother's stitches were, how uniform and regular—even when she was very old.

A buggy jingles down the road outside, breaking the peace and quiet. Emma looks up. "I can keep quilting for hours," she says. That's okay, I say. I can keep drawing for hours. The clock chimes. We keep on.

Emma and Amos have been married for only six months. They had many guests at their wedding, and it took all winter to visit each family. "It took a while, but it was a special time for us," they tell me.

I show Amos the finished drawings. "Are you staying for supper?" he asks. "Could I take the drawing to the photocopier where I work?"

Ten minutes later I'm sitting in a furniture showroom, trying out various oak rocking chairs while Amos is knocking out the copies and laying them across the office floor—linoleum, of course; the Amish don't normally use carpet.

✦ ✦

Sadie has spent all day sewing quilts with her grandmother, mother, and daughter, and a friend and her daughter. On average, an Amish woman will complete a quilt every month. It's usually finished off at a church meeting on the first Wednesday of the month. The quilts they're making today are for Christian Aid. They're to be sent to Romania.

Everyone has left, but Sadie and her daughter Ruth carry on a little in the growing darkness, among the quilt

Emma sits at home, quietly quilting a Double Wedding Ring design, a mix of cotton and acrylic with a polyester-fiber filling.

patches strewn across the floor. Ruth stands on one end of the quilt as her mother pulls on the opposite end, bringing it up taut.

"When I see a piece of material," Sadie says, "I can't leave it. A lot is given to us by people who know we're doing this for Romania."

It's Sadie's birthday today. "Oh, we don't do anything special," she says.

They did pick flowers, though. Ruth shows me a crayon drawing she made of herself and her mother as they headed home with bunches of purple lilac. In the middle of the kitchen table is a jar holding the blossoms.

We begin to tidy up, putting the different sizes of squares in boxes and the off-cuts in a trash box. It's getting dark. Sadie lights one of the gas lamps. Being accustomed to brightly lit rooms, I have a hard time seeing the squares.

"Some years ago my daughter's boyfriend got her an old quilt for $100 at an auction," Alvin tells me. "He gave it to my daughter, who brought it home to show me. When I saw it I couldn't believe it. It was a Center Diamond, deep blues and reds, the finest wool, real museum quality. I knew it was worth over $8000. I told her just to put it away and say nothing. Later, when they got married, they sold it and used the money to put down on a house."

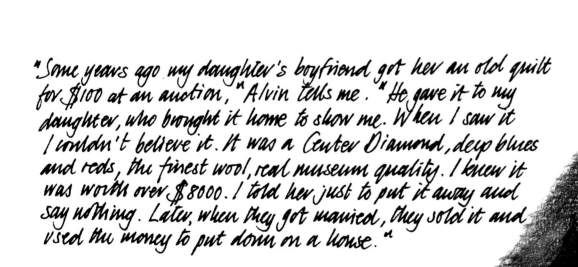

HEADING HOME

Now it's evening. The shadows lengthen and the breeze drops as I sit by a creek, painting a fallen tree. I've been at it an hour or so when a farmer strolls across the fields on the opposite bank, moving his cattle toward the farm. He sees me and calls over: "Have you caught anything yet?"

I'm not fishing, I explain. I'm painting a picture.

He looks puzzled. "Why don't you take a photograph? People come here fishing for trout," he explains. "I'd like to get over to talk to you, but I guess I can't. I'll walk down and see you later."

Since I've been here, a Mennonite buggy has arrived and parked by the bridge. A young couple sit on the bank, fishing in the creek. She wears a pink dress; he has a shirt to match. The midges are biting, the fish are rising, and within twenty minutes the sun will have set. As I pack up to go, five large horses trundle across the field and down to the creek to drink.

◆ ◆

I pack my painting things away and prepare to leave. It's my last evening among the Amish this spring. The sun is dipping below the horizon. Ruth comes over with a bouquet of wildflowers she's just picked. I say my farewells.

"Stay longer next time," they say. I take the flowers to the car and put them carefully onto the seat.

SUMMER

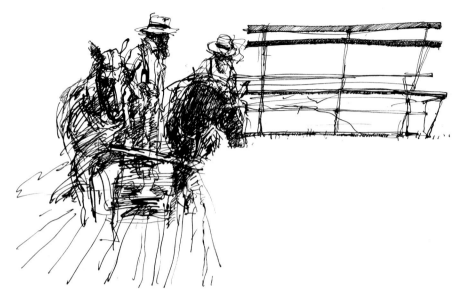

HARVESTING WHEAT

Gideon shows me the old McCormick-Deering binder and explains how it works. Then we go to a field of wheat that has just been put into rows of shocks to dry in the hot sun. He shows me how to take up, hold, and stack the shocks. A smile crosses his face as he explains, "I just took a notion to do it. That was wonderful. It brought back so many memories."

Gideon, who used to be a farmer, is now a bookbinder. Farming has become a less and less viable means of earning a living for the Amish. In 1940 the population of Lancaster County was 200,000; today it's closer to 500,000. Farmland has become too expensive for what it can produce.

There is comparatively little wheat grown today. The price is still about the same as it was twenty years ago, and there's a lot of hard work involved in harvesting it—cutting, binding, shocking, and threshing.

❖ ❖

Out in the field, the McCormick-Deering binder, first manufactured more than one hundred years ago, is being pulled around by two black Percheron horses. Things are not going well. There are interruptions every fifteen minutes as one part after another fails. Last stop was to fix the binding twine. Now it's the canvas bed.

Emmanuel and Eli had hoped to finish this field today, but now it's clear they won't. The canvas bed has slackened off and must be tightened by removing one of the wooden cross-slats.

Eli walks back across the fields to fetch more tools—a pair of pliers and a hacksaw. When he returns, he saws the rivets off the cross-slat, passes them to me to put in the tool box, and tightens the canvas.

They start binding again, working their way along the rows of wheat. Ten minutes later, everything comes to a halt once more. This time the binder is taken off the field. The rest of the wheat will have to wait until tomorrow, weather permitting.

In the meantime, Emmanuel and Eli stack the shocks on the field to dry. They pick up one bundle under each arm and drop them together, standing the shocks upright. It's very difficult to pick up the second bundle while holding onto the first one. The wheat scratches your bare arms.

"I wish I'd worn my long-sleeved shirt," Emmanuel says with a rueful smile. I noticed earlier that Eli had gone in to change his shirt for a long-sleeved dark-blue one before shocking the wheat.

The shocks are stacked in groups of eight to ten in rows across the field so air can pass through them and speed the drying process. They must stand at least a few days in good sunny weather before threshing can begin.

◆ ◆

Next day, the children, from the youngest to the oldest, are loading shocks of wheat onto the cart in the hot evening air. Again there are problems—the horses keep bolting up the field. They're brought back around but are still uneasy. Then, when they seem calm again, the end flies off one of the forks. The clatter sends them bolting up the field once more.

Eventually someone realizes the horses have been hitched the wrong way. The leader must always be on the right-hand side as the team comes toward you. Once that's been fixed, we head back onto the field. We load the shocks with the heads toward the center of the cart, laying them vertically along its length and horizontally to fill in the middle.

"Who's the lead rider here?" asks Emmanuel, standing by a pair of his beloved horses. He calls across the field to a group of young boys: "Raymond! You rider?" Raymond runs over and clambers on top of the lead horse. Completely at ease, he catches hold of the reins and moves the team forward, keeping the cart alongside the shocks of wheat.

The boys tell me they sometimes leave the middle shocks out to create a hole in the center, then cover it lightly. When their fathers come to unload, they fall through into the hole and can't get out until the majority of the load has been forked off the cart. The boys all find this extremely funny. I've not heard their fathers' side of the story, though.

Two young girls arrive on the field in an open buggy pulled by a miniature horse. They bring supplies of fresh, cold water. Then an empty cart pulls up, driven by three small children—the relief squad. Their combined ages can't be more than twenty.

◆ ◆

Back at the farm, where the threshing machine has been set up, they're having problems. One of the belts has just broken. The boys tell me that last year the main belt

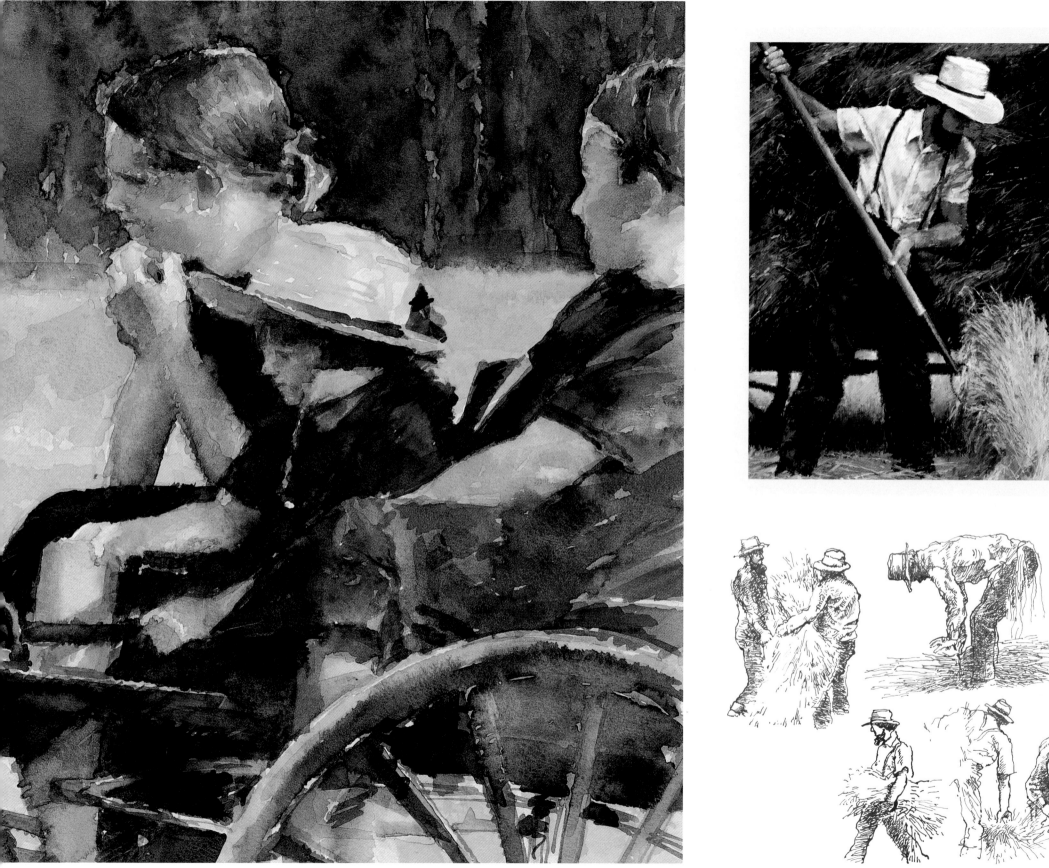

snapped: "It was like a rifle crack!" It flew off into the corn, some considerable distance away. The boys were loading a cart in another field when they heard the sound. Their mules bolted with a full load. "We were sure the load would turn over. Every year something goes wrong and we end up having to fix it," says one of the boys.

More boys are in the barn, stacking straw bales and joking loudly about the various merits of horses as compared to mules. Another load is brought in, the horse running up the short incline at the entrance. Suddenly the barn is filled with noises—the heavy metal wheels, the creaking timbers of the old cart, bales flying off, hooves scraping on the ground, horses rushing past, and everyone calling to put a block under the back wheel to stop the cart from sliding back out of the barn. The impression is one of organized chaos. Everybody lends a hand.

I help with forking the shocks of wheat off the cart and into the thresher. The wheat comes out through the top pipe into a large container, while straw bales are fed into the barn and stacked.

An Amish woman comes over to talk. "The children love to join in the threshing, but one mustn't worry too much about them," she tells me. Then she heads back into the house to finish preparing the threshers' supper. "They work so hard. They'll be hungry."

The sun is setting now. The men carry on trying to repair the thresher, and the children are sitting around in groups. Some of the younger ones are climbing on the threshing machine or to the top of the carts, which are still loaded high with wheat. Below, three kittens seem to mimic them, rolling around together in the grass.

Later, I hear a story of harvesting disaster. If a load of wheat is drawn up too close to the belts and pulleys of the threshing machine when it's running, there's a danger that the load will catch fire. "That wheat's just ready to go up!" Emmanuel says. On one occasion, apparently, it did just that, and the fire spread quickly through the load. The cart was driven quickly away from the thresher and the other carts of wheat. As they drove it out of the way and around the field, the fire took greater hold. Flames rushed through the shocks of wheat, fanned by the wind blowing around the moving cart. They managed to put out the fire just as the "English" fire brigade arrived.

Sitting on the grass, drawing the threshing machine. The men have just finished lunch. They stand silently at the back, gazing intently at the drawing. Eventually they drift away to begin work again. One man leans over pointing at my picture. "You've done that before."

THE ART CRITIC

I sit on a pallet outside the barn, painting Samuel's horses. My sketchbook is propped up on a wooden plank. Emmanuel and Alan are moving lumber behind me with a forklift. Elmer's loading wood shavings for bedding into a cart. The shavings snow down on my painting. A dog dozes with his head in my lap, and little Isaac is testing the dry paintbrushes on my trousers.

"It's pretty good," Isaac says, placing a hand on the painting to see if it's dry, "but sometimes kind of scribbly."

MILKING

It's been well over a hundred degrees in the fields. As I walk back to the farm, the cows are emerging slowly from the cool, dark recesses of a large covered shed that has been their shelter from the burning midafternoon sun. Now it's evening milking time, and they make their way to the dairy, where cool air is wafted by fans suspended from the ceiling, driven by an elaborate system of pulleys. It's cooler here—almost refreshing—but the thermometer still reads eighty-five.

Three children are busily at work. They carry the milkers to each cow, plug one end into the air line, and connect the other to the four teats. The milk starts flowing. The children remain busy. They move a group of cows that have finished out of the dairy and prepare for the next batch.

In the background, a younger boy wrestles with a large broom, cleaning the floor between two rows of contented cows. The broom must be at least eighteen inches taller than he.

Amid all of this activity, a three-year-old boy on a tricycle is riding about, making race-car noises and swerving around his older brothers.

When the individual milkers are full, they're hauled over to a bigger container, the sputnik, which is wheeled down the center aisle. The sputnik, in its turn, is wheeled back and emptied into the main tank in the cool of the dairy.

As I prepare to leave, Samuel calls to me from inside: "Don't go yet. I've got something to tell you."

I wander back into the dairy, down the line of milking cows—Judy, Ruth, Amanda, Sandy, Douna, Calico, Gene, Arlene, Clover, Jolly, Betty, Geneva, Verna, Polly, Lolly, Girtie, Alta, Ginger, Freda, Ellen, Carrie, Louise, Cathy, Gail, Cookie, Eva, Violet, Jan, Gwen, Robin, and Vickie—thirty-one in all.

At the end of the line sits a baby in a buggy. "I knew there was something I hadn't told you," Samuel says. "We had our first baby since you were last here. This is Michael. He's four months now."

MAKING HAY

Alfalfa is the best for cows. They won't go without it. What they need is corn, grain, and alfalfa—the Holy Trinity," Emmanuel says.

Alfalfa is resown every fourth year. In the first year, the crop is not so good. The second year is the best. After that the weeds start to get into it, but with a strong root system the crop is able to withstand extremes of temperature. Last winter the temperature dropped to minus ten. Today, as the first cut is being taken off a crop that was sown this spring, the heat on the field is intense—around a hundred and ten.

With the water in my paint pot evaporating by the minute, I try to draw Elias and his team as they work their way slowly to the center of the field, cutting the sweet-smelling alfalfa into swaths. Barn swallows dive into the field all about them to feed on the newly released insect hordes. In five weeks' time this crop will have grown again and will be ready for its second cut.

After the grass is cut it's raked into rows. Later, after a day or so of good weather, the tedding machine is put to work to turn it over so it can dry thoroughly. Then it's raked into rows once more and made ready for the baler.

When to bale hay seems to be critical. If it's too dry it loses its protein and is not good for the milk yield. Sometimes they'll wait until evening to bale it, so there's

"Take the world as it is, not as it ought to be."
German proverb.

some dew on it. The first cutting yields the greatest quantity, but it's too stemmy. Quality and price go up on each successive cutting, but quantity goes down. A mix of cuttings is given when feeding.

Mae, the golden retriever, has been following the horses as they pull the cutting machine around the field. Now, feeling the burning heat, she retreats to the shade of an empty hay cart and eventually back to the barn for water. I follow, glancing as I pass at the thermometer. Even here, in the cool shade on an outside wall of the barn, it reads ninety-five.

I remember standing in freezing temperatures here in February, watching as they covered the ice-encrusted surface of this same field with manure to make it ready for sowing alfalfa in the spring. Mae chased the horses then, too. It seems another age.

Mae cools off in the shade of an empty hay cart.

CULTIVATING

I'm drawing Samuel as he patiently works his way along the rows of green corn. In early May he was harvesting rye grass out of this same field, but now, ten weeks later, the scene looks totally different. The green corn is quickly gaining height.

Today, Samuel uses the McCormick-Deering cultivator to pull out the weed pickle and morning glory. "I sprayed it with insecticide but I still have to cultivate it," he explains. Without regular cultivating, the weed would grow as high as the crop, strangle it, and halt the harvesting.

Samuel's father goes out every day to measure the corn crop. With delight he tells me it's growing one and a quarter inches every day. Sunshine, rain, good soil, and good farming have made for a good crop, he tells me.

"But you know what they say the best crop of them all is? The next generation."

CORN SILAGE

The perspective of the field is accentuated by the rows of stalks, cut evenly a couple of inches above the ground, converging toward the horizon. Years ago this crop was cut by hand, requiring many men to labor for long hours. Today, Abner, an eleven-year-old boy, drives the harvester as his father, grandfather, and uncle work at stacking the cut corn on the back.

His uncle, Jonas, says the corn is still a little green for harvesting. "Could ripen more, but we need to take some now, since we're getting low on feed."

Abner steers the horses at a fast walking pace, always looking behind him to make sure the binder is in the right position for taking on the corn. He wants to work with horses when he finishes school. In fact, he prefers working on the farm to being at school.

At the back of the cart, Emmanuel puts his arm through one sleeve of his jacket to protect himself from being torn and scratched as the corn comes off the binder. Over by the silo, another full load rumbles into the yard. The mules are brought to a halt nearby. Unloading starts again, and

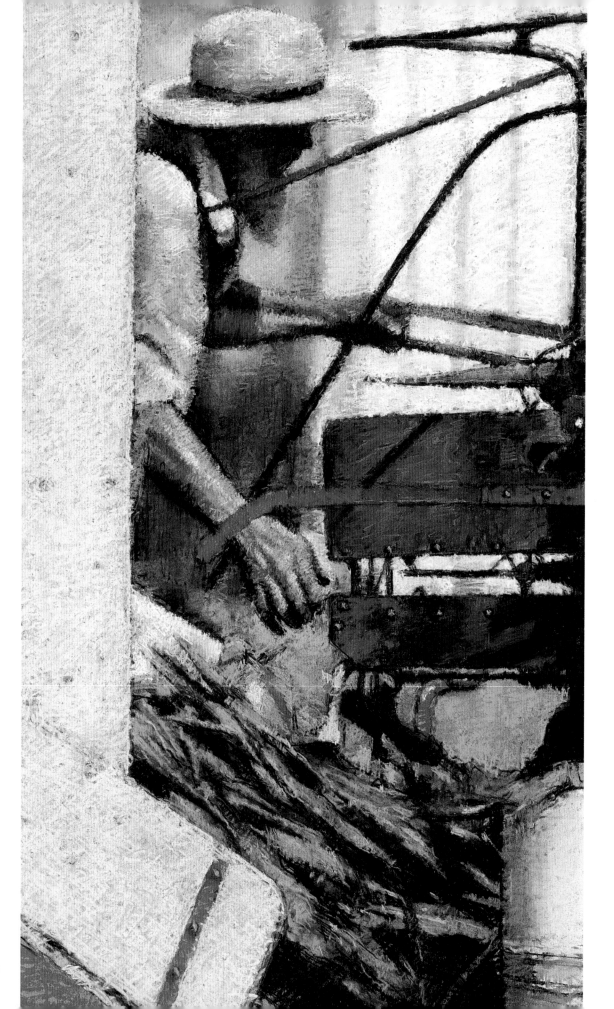

the green corn is thrown into the chopper and blown up into the silo.

The scene is a flurry of noise, dust, and hard physical labor—sweat-soaked shirts, powerful arms with straining sinews, bits of dust and corn flying in the air, deafening diesel-engine noise, and intermittent calls to the mules to move forward or backward to keep the position of the load alongside the chopper.

"I always wanted to be a farmer," Emmanuel tells me later. "I can work and be with my family at the same time."

They've been making silage all day, and now the silo is full. But there's a problem: Emmanuel has run out of silage covers, and each silo must be covered before it rains and the corn spoils. It must be done soon, too: "I won't be able to get in the silo tomorrow because of the methane gas. Too dangerous." We make it to the store just before it closes, and we're back to the farm before it rains.

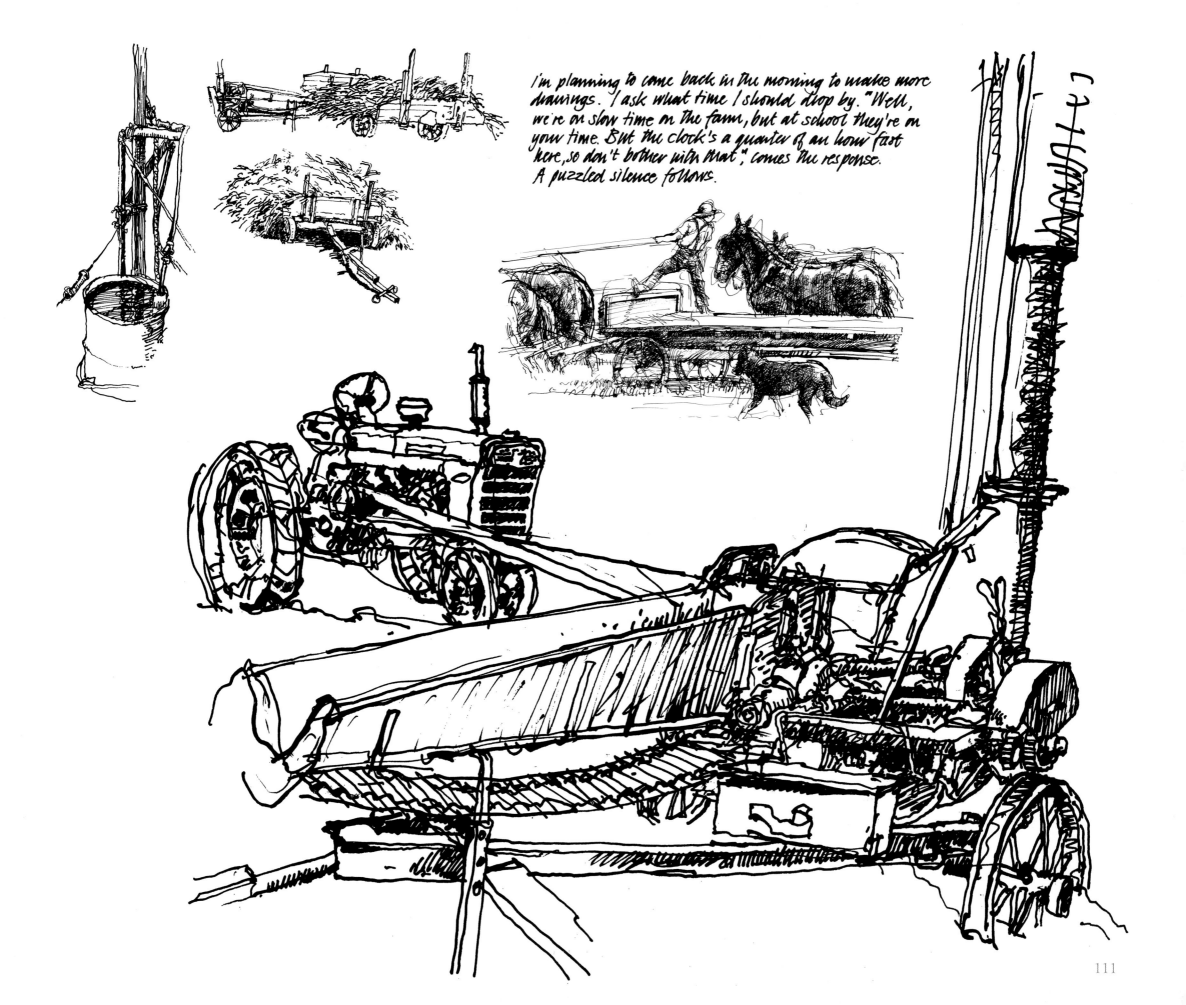

I'm planning to come back in the morning to make more drawings. I ask what time I should drop by. "Well, we're on slow time on the farm, but at school they're on your time. But the clock's a quarter of an hour fast here, so don't bother with that", comes the response. A puzzled silence follows.

CUTTING AND SPEARING TOBACCO

The tobacco plants reach above Jonas's waist as he stands among the crop. An "English" neighbor comes across the field with food and drink. "Have you ever seen such big tobacco?" he asks. "Have you ever seen anyone work as hard as Jonas?"

Jonas pours oil on the blade of his tobacco cutter, then spits into both hands and rubs them together. The cutter has a long handle with a curved blade at the bottom, like a garden pruner. He cuts eight rows of tobacco at a time, then leaves the cuttings to dry and wilt in the sun before spearing them a couple of days later. "We cut it and leave it, spear it and leave it, load it and leave it, then finally hang it and leave it," Jonas explains.

The greener the plant, the heavier. Leaving it lets it wilt and lose some weight. You can see the moisture beginning to disappear, to evaporate and sink as you look inside the upended, cut stalk. Also, the greener the plant, the more easily it will break when handled, so wilting helps in making it more supple.

Last night's rainfall still lies in puddles in the hollows of leaves cut a couple of days ago. "It's like a plate," Jonas says, picking up one leaf. "It just keeps the water. There's nowhere for it to go." The wooden laths for spearing are pulled off the wagon in bundles and dropped on top of the cut leaves. "Must go and help with some housework before we unload another cart," says Jonas.

Later, he's back in the field, straightening the tip of his spear by kneeling down and banging it between two stones. Then he begins spearing four to five leaves onto each lath. The day is still hazy and humid after the rain. The moist leaves stain Jonas's clothes as he works. Gradually he becomes camouflaged among the tobacco plants, his once-clean shirt taking on the same yellow tint as the wilting leaves. "It doesn't feel much like a tobacco-spearing day," he remarks quietly.

I've been drawing Jonas for most of the day, as he methodically works his way along the rows of tobacco. He stops cutting, walks over, and whispers to me: "We have an audience". I look over to the edge of the field where a family have been busy videoing me - drawing Jonas - cutting tobacco.

HANGING TOBACCO

Another load of tobacco leaves is run up the incline and into the barn. The back wheel of the cart is blocked quickly to stop it from rolling back. The wagon is full of leaves hanging on yard-long wooden laths.

When the loads are brought in off the fields, the wagons are left standing a while so the leaves can settle before being unloaded. The horses are unhitched and carefully

backed out between the cart and the barn door. Then the men move the loaded cart farther into the barn so it's in the correct position for unloading.

Later, three of us start unloading the laths of speared leaves. Elias is above, balancing in the rafters. Jonas, Elias's father, is just below him, and I'm in the cart. I lift each lath, placing one hand in the center and the other at the end. Jonas takes the opposite end as I offer it up. He passes it to Elias, who quickly stacks it high up under the roof. Eventually the layers of drying leaves will be three or more deep. It takes us about half an hour to unload.

For the next load, Elias selects an even higher beam, about fifty feet up, immediately under the roof of the massive barn. Jonas balances on the beam below, and Martha, Elias's wife, joins us to stand on a makeshift plank placed between a lower strut and the cart. I again take my place on the cart. We silently pass each lath up to the roof, where it will dry for a few months.

What began as a high, open ceiling, a dark brown mesh of cross beams, is gradually transformed into a low canopy of yellow-green, close-hanging, pointed leaves. Within a day or two of hanging, the formerly bright-green leaves begin to change color, from yellow to a deeper brown.

The cattle are coming in for milking below as Elias climbs up through the loft and balances his way across the narrow beams and up into the roof space. He selects the next place from which to start hanging the leaves.

As I pass another lath up to Jonas, I look up at the soles of Elias's heavy boots. I notice how his hat brushes the bottom of the hanging leaves. "Yes, you've got the job. Next we'll have you up here on the beams," he calls down to me.

When the leaves are taken down in the winter, they'll have dried out and become much lighter, so the laths can be taken down three at a time. But now, just after harvesting, the leaves are heavy. The laths must be hung one at a time—to lift any more would be too difficult.

The rows of leaves hang four deep in the roof. Elias is high up among the top row. I see only his feet balancing across the high beam. Jonas is just below, straddling two beams and bending double to take the laths as Martha and I pass them up to him. He grasps one end of each lath,

then turns nimbly to offer the other end to Elias. Lath by lath, the cart is emptied. The leaves that remain are gathered and thrown up into the roof, where they stick to the hanging leaves.

"Dad's getting a bit stiff to leap up and down on the beams," Elias says to me later. "When he was young he could do three beams at once." Jonas is in his mid-seventies now. Having watched his strength and agility all day, I can't think of a reply. I just smile back.

We ride out to the tobacco fields for another load. Two mules pull the cart. Jonas sits on the metal seat up front, holding the reins. I stand by his side, leaning on the rail, feeling the unforgiving metal wheels beneath us as we roll along the paved road.

In the winter, when there's time between jobs, the farmers strip tobacco, making the leaves into bales, ready for the auction. It has to be the right kind of day—a damp day. If it's too dry the leaves will be too brittle and they'll crumble.

Today it's very humid, and now we hear the sounds of distant thunder. With two carts loaded, Elias and Jonas head off into the fields again. They'd like to bring in another load before it rains. Before they go, they hitch up a load that has been standing and pull it inside. Another crack of thunder is heard. This time it's nearer. The storm's headed our way.

Jonas goes off to get some old plastic sacks. "Have you got something to keep off the rain?" he asks me. "We won't need anything—our shirts are soaking wet already." Soaked with sweat, he means—their shirts have become translucent with wetness, clinging to their backs.

In the fields, two carts are hitched up. The back one is loaded first. One man on each side, Elias and Jonas load quickly. They call to the mules to pull forward, then to stop: "Yip Kate! Whoa!"

The metal wheels dig deeper into the red earth, the mules straining as the second cart is loaded. Then it's unhitched and the mules are turned around to begin the next row of speared, wilting leaves. The full load is covered with the plastic to protect it from the coming storm.

This is the last of this year's tobacco crop. Now it's all safe and dry before the rain.

THE PRODUCE
MARKET

We're driving along the lanes in an open buggy on a beautiful summer morning, heading for the produce market. It feels so much better traveling this way—slowly, looking across the fields, with more time to chat as the breeze plays on your face. Ruth sees some miniature horses in the fields. She'd like to have one.

I try my hand at the reins, and we seem to be going along fine until we descend a slight incline and start speeding up. I pass the reins back to Emmanuel. My expertise in horsemanship has been rapidly exceeded.

Emmanuel comments on the sorry state of my sunburned legs and the blisters on my hands. I spent yesterday forking shocks of hay onto the thresher. He must think we "English" are a fairly pathetic lot, but of course he doesn't say so. He simply remarks that *he* couldn't hold a pencil for as long as I do.

After we arrive, I sense that someone is standing next to me. I look around, and it's Joshua, smiling as usual. What time did you get here? I ask. "Oh, about eight o'clock. We've got a load of peppers." Where's your dad? "Back at the farm."

It's now nine o'clock. The lines of horse-drawn carts loaded with produce wait their turn to come under the auctioneer's hammer. The sun is already strong, so some of the loads are covered with sheets to be taken off when the carts are brought into the shade of the auctioneer's shed.

As we leave the market, Ruth sees some fresh pretzels. She'd like to have one—they don't cost as much as miniature horses. We spread on the mustard.

HARVESTING POTATOES

Emmanuel and Sadie plow their garden plot to harvest potatoes. Sadie leads the mule, Pete. She smiles at me: "I always get the awkward one to lead." Emmanuel's stance alters as he leans on the plow to apply more pressure. "Still can't find the row," he says. Then quietly, "It's in there somewhere."

They work their way down the rows, collecting the unearthed potatoes in large baskets to be carried inside and laid out on the cellar floor. The cut or split ones are used first. As Emmanuel and Sadie collect the potatoes, little Ruth picks gourds, gathering them in her skirt and dropping them into a basket at the end of the row.

"I planted the gourds here years ago," her mother explains. "They just keep coming up. You can't do anything with them. They're just for decoration. Last year Ruth put some in a box out front to sell, and someone left a dollar."

After supper we're all back in the field picking potatoes. The plow turns up each row, then we work our way down. The girls kick the newly turned warm earth with their bare feet to expose the hidden potatoes. Occasionally, a surreptitious potato is aimed at an unsuspecting brother or sister.

Pulling up weeds as she goes, Linda calls over to me: "Don't draw the weeds in." The small, bruised, and green potatoes are put in one basket, to be eaten first. The big ones go in the other basket.

When the truck is full, we carefully move the load around the house to the cellar at the back. Alan pulls the cart from the front. I stay at the back, steadying the load. I watch his bare feet walking across the rough gravel. We lay the potatoes on the cool concrete floor of the cellar. When we're done, there's talk of bringing in another load of firewood.

GARDENING

Sadie and her friend Barbi, who has come to help, are working on the garden, mowing lawns, tidying flower beds, clipping sides, cutting back weeds with a motorized trimmer, and sweeping the paths and the yard.

Ruth is playing with an old broom. Now she wants me to play—she on her tricycle, I on her scooter. We race from the top of the farmyard, past the big barn doors, around a sharp corner, then down the slope of the yard to the dog kennel. This is great fun, but after a dozen or so races I go back to sitting on the cart and drawing. Ruth comes to sit by me, quietly holding out her cupped hands to collect the shavings as I sharpen my pencil.

Last year I gave Ruth a children's picture book that I illustrated, about a horse that pulls a canal boat. Her mother told me how Ruth had been playing, pretending to be the horse and pulling her plastic sled across the puddles. Now we are due for a further episode, as Ruth pretends to be a horse and puts on a harness to pull her wagon.

As I sit on the cart in the corner of the yard I am aware of the stillness. A slight breeze sets off the windmill. The blades turn, and down below the water pump's piston moves up and down. Ruth sits right by my side, holding a cat upside down, its front paws balancing on my sketch pad. I keep drawing.

"I like to do garden work on Fridays," Sadie tells me, "so it's tidy for Sunday. I like to be outside as much as possible in the good weather."

CANNING

Grandmother, mother, and daughter sit outside, under the shade of a tree, at a large table with all the paraphernalia for making applesauce. This afternoon they have made precisely 249 pints. They put the sugar in without bothering to weigh, just tasting as they make each batch. "You never know how sweet or sour the apples are going to be," comes the explanation.

As I look over more baskets brimming with apples and wonder where they all came from, Martha turns to me and points: "They're all from that orchard there."

♦ ♦

For canning, pickles, beets, and radishes are washed in the washing machine, which is driven by air compression. "It brings them up cleaner than scrubbing," Elias explains. He shows me his radish-washing machine. It's a rust-colored revolving drum with water jets inside. He opens the trapdoor and we descend the steps from the workshop to the cellar, where he keeps the various diesel engines that power everything in sight. "This we call the power house," he tells me.

We check that the pressure of the water in the revolving drum is correct. Pointing to the dial, Elias yells in my ear above the engine noise: "I've increased it to 2,000 PSI. Leave it an hour. That should wash them. Even the President's got a jar of this radish."

THE WATERMELON HARVEST

Three types of melon are grown on the farm: Sangria, which is oblong in shape; King of Hearts, a seedless, round variety; and Crimson Sweet, which fetches the best price.

"I'll tell you the way to eat them," Emmanuel says. "Take a piece and squeeze a little lemon on it. That's good for you.

"We've been harvesting for over three weeks, but in the first two weeks not much came. Then, this week, they've all come at once. We have to pick them all today and tomorrow to get them to the market for this week. I hope it's still hot. People don't want watermelon when it's cloudy. By next week it'll be too late."

Most of the family is involved: Alan and Elmer, the two eldest boys; Linda and Michael, the twins; Isaac (asleep among the melons); and the baby in her buggy.

Alan shows me how to bend over to pick up a melon and tap it with my hand to hear if it's ringing hollow and not flat. The underside should be a strong yellow color. The tendril that's connected to the melon should be dry

and withered. You clean off the soil from the underside by wiping the melon with leaves, then carefully place it in the cart. If the melons knock together, they could split open.

With a full load the horses find it difficult to pull the cart back to the farm. We all help by pushing from behind as we cross the field. On returning, we feed the melons that have split to the animals, who all seem to relish them.

We stop for a break and sit outside at the table in the garden. We lower our heads to say a short, silent prayer before beginning to eat. The meal consists of eggplant sandwiches with homemade ketchup, tomatoes, pickles, pretzels, milk to drink, and, of course, watermelon to finish. We fork out great chunks of crimson-pink flesh from the segments we cut with a large kitchen knife. Mae, the golden retriever, readily eats up any pieces that fall her way.

Back at the farm we lay the melons in the shade of a barn, arranging them by shape and size. Jack, the lead mule ("I don't know how old he is, could be thirty years . . ."), takes a bite out of a melon on the large round pile. "Well," says Emmanuel, "we stopped for something to eat, and he didn't."

After the break, Emmanuel goes off to feed the cattle while the boys drive back into the fields on their own to start reloading the empty cart.

◆ ◆

We are riding back from the fields with our last load of the day. It's getting darker. We were barely able to see the last melons as we loaded them up. I'm riding at the back of the cart. Emmanuel, who's up front, calls over to me: "Look—they're still picking peppers up there."

I can just make out the silhouettes of his neighbors on the ridge above. The boys call out to them in greeting, and their calls are returned. The banter continues until we're at too great a distance to be heard.

In the pitch-blackness we arrive in the farmyard. Leaving the cart and its contents to be unloaded and sorted around five in the morning, we go into the wash house to clean up. Back in the house, Sadie lights a couple of gas lanterns as we all take off our shoes and place them in a row. Hats are hung on pegs above the shoes.

"With God let all things begin, With God let all things come to rest."

Amish Bible bookplate 1845

Emmanuel goes upstairs to change into his best clothes while I wait to drive him and some neighbors to an evening of hymn-singing practice. As we wait, the conversation turns to me. They don't see what's so interesting for me to draw around here. For them it's just everyday, just normal. I tell them that at home we haven't farmed like this in nearly a century. It's wonderful for me to see that this lifestyle has been preserved. You shouldn't ever change, I tell them.

Through the lantern light I can see their faces looking at me. They smile. "No," one of them says, "we don't intend to."

129